Paula ~
We are so happy to
be here celebrating your
New Beginning! Your strength
and inspiration is ALL-Star amazing*
Conrad Courage!!
Love, Your "Cali-Cousins"
Caren, Carla & Cathrin

WE ARE CUBS FANS

AN UNOFFICIAL JOURNAL OF BASEBALL's BEST FANS - VOLUME #1

To Paula - A true Cubs Fan! Go Cubs Go—
Will Byington

ORIGINAL PHOTOGRAPHY AND STORIES COMPILED BY

WILL BYINGTON

There are not enough pages in this book to thank everyone who has helped me and supported this project. Thank you to my friends who have joined me at games and supported my photography adventure. Thank you to those who have smiled, posed, and laughed in front of my camera or submitted a personal story for this book. I look forward to seeing you all around the neighborhood.

This book is dedicated to my parents – Hunter and Barbara Byington.
Without them, their love and support... none of this would have been possible.

ISBN# 978-0-615-21797-0

For more information, please contact Will Byington Photography (www.willbyington.com) by mail, phone or e-mail.

Will Byington Photography
P.O. Box 5397
Naperville, IL 60567-5397

(312) 498-6444 office

wearecubsfans@gmail.com

ISBN 978-0-615-21797-0

52995

9 780615 217970

Day in and day out, 81 days a year, 40,000 or more fans descend upon a baseball shrine named Wrigley Field. Bordered by the streets of Clark, Addison, Waveland and Sheffield, it is known as "The Friendly Confines." Win or lose, rain or shine, fans trek from near and far to watch some baseball, bask in the summer sun and cheer on the boys in blue, forgetting for a short while the world around them. Some of the fans are young, born into a lifetime of fandom... Others are old, wishing and hoping to just see one World Series win... an event that has not happened in their lifetime... since 1908 in fact. For some, the trek to the ballpark is a means of life... a job, a resource to earn a living. For others, it is a passion... from the moment they entered the concourse as a child, smelling the scents of the grass, the food and the beer and hearing the sounds of the old organ and the crack of the bat... it has been embedded in their hearts through joy and pain. This book is dedicated to those who believe. This book is their story.

Will Byington, June 2008

WE ARE CUBS FANS

"Eighty-five percent of the world is working.
The other fifteen is out here
to watch day baseball."
— Lee Elia, Chicago Cubs Manager, 1983

I love the fact that we Cub fans are all tied to a collective belief, "One day, will be our day." Whether you are a fan who saw the Cubs lose the series in 1945, or you witnessed the collapse in 1969 or felt the heartbreak of '84 and '03. We all still BELIEVE one day we will win it all.

There is just as much faith, hope, and love, at Wrigley Field as there is in Churches, Temples, or Synagogues.

JUST BELIEVE

Matt Liston

"Chasing October: A fan's crusade"

I love to get to Wrigley about 2 hours before game time, so I can walk through the concourse as the vendors are preparing for the day. There's nothing like the sweat smell of those onions right when they hit the grill!   I love watching Batting Practice & I love the buzz of the crowd as the stadium fills with CUBS FANS. I love when those fans stand to cheer on the pitcher with 2 outs & a 3-2 count - in the 2nd inning.

I love keeping score with my wife, drinking beers with my friends, singing during the stretch, and watching the Closer slam the door on another W... usually after hitting the first batter then giving up a base hit and another walk to load the bases before miraculously squeaking out of it. I love singing GO CUBS GO! and then going to Murphy's to drink & relive the whole thing...

And I love that it's time again, to head back to Wrigley to smell those onions grilling and cheer on our CUBS!
   Still Chasing October!

Chris (L) and Matt (R), Directors, with a fan of their movie "Chasing October"

WE ARE CUBS FANS

WE ARE CUBS FANS

WE ARE CUBS FANS

WHAT THE CUBS MEAN TO ME...

When all else failed me, for the last 82 ~~84~~ years I have always had the Cubs to carry me through

Gladys Nunley

Gladys Nunley

WE ARE CUBS FANS

The Cubs are a symbol of hope. I live at the corner of Sheffield and Waveland and have been fortunate to see many good times in Wrigleyville. The persistence and optimism that radiates from the stands is palpable. Wrigley Field is my happy place, and catching a ball game there is one of my favorite things to do. Each season brings a renewed energy for the return of a playoff run and the hope that this will be the year the Cubs are crowned champions!

– Derek Mulder

WE ARE CUBS FANS

WE ARE CUBS FANS

For Chicago Cub fans, the baseball season is a manic -depressive hayride.
For Cardinal fans it's just a hayride.

There's always next year? Is that what you're wondering?

You could depend on next year back in 1908 when Teddy Roosevelt
had the quaint notion that Americans should be getting a square deal.
You could depend on next year when the first flying machine couldn't
get much farther than the next sand dune. But this is 2008. One hundred
next years later. There is no more bitter falsehood than the phrase,
"there's always next year."

So let us all live this season like the runaway locomotive, Carlos Zambrano,
rounds third base. No thought of the past, no thought of the future.

Only this: I am not stopping because the good century begins now.

Lin Brehmer,
Mornings 93.1 WXRT-FM

WE ARE CUBS FANS

WE ARE CUBS FANS

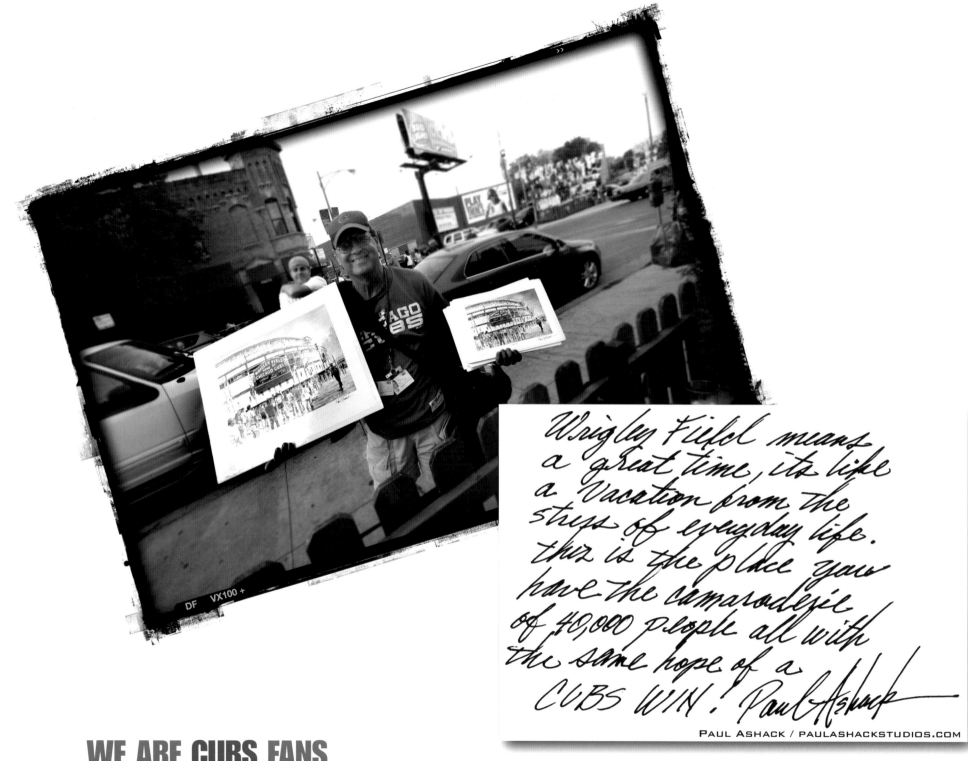

Wrigley Field means a great time, its like a vacation from the stress of everyday life. this is the place you have the camaraderie of 40,000 people all with the same hope of a CUBS WIN! Paul Ashack

PAUL ASHACK / PAULASHACKSTUDIOS.COM

WE ARE CUBS FANS

DF   VX100 +

WE ARE CUBS FANS

WE ARE CUBS FANS

CHICAGO SUN-TIMES
THE BRIGHT ONE

RICK TELANDER
Sports Columnist

April '08
(100 years)

1969 almost killed me—
as a Cubs Fan and a young
human being. But having
the Cubs **NOT WIN** links
everybody into a collective
stew of yearning, sadness,
and beer-drinking. AND ain't that **life**?

Rick T.

350 NORTH ORLEANS STREET, CHICAGO, ILLINOIS 60654

PARTY LIKE IT'S 1908
NEXT YEAR DAY

WE ARE CUBS FANS

DF   VX100 +   ››

WE ARE CUBS FANS

Chug Chug, Heckler mascot

WE ARE CUBS FANS

WHAT THE CUBS MEAN TO ME...

Either sitting in a seat at Wrigley, or sitting in my recliner at home... for 6 months out of the year, the best 3+ hours of my spring & summer days are spent watching the Cubs. Living 700 miles from Wrigley Field means I get to see the team in person only a handful of times a season... so looking forward in anticipation to those fun-filled Cubs baseball weekends is what gets me through those long, long winter months. That's what being a fan of the Chicago Cubs means to me.
                                    — Jeremy

WE ARE CUBS FANS

SEWARD ALASKA LOVES DA CUBS

WE ARE CUBS FANS

going to Wrigley Field for a Cubs game
has always felt magical to me. each and
every time there is a memorable experience
for me! My first Cubs memories start with
my family taking me to ball games when i was
little — when i believed andre dawson was
"made for me", simply because his jersey number
was #8, and i was 8 years old at the time!
Being the dreamer i was, i wanted to marry
"the Hawk", see the Cubbies WIN it all, and
even sing the national anthem at Wrigley
one day.
   Well... my name is yet to be dawson, but
on September 10, 2007, at a sold out
Cardinals game, my dream came true to
finally step on the field and sing our country's
Star Spangled Banner at Wrigley Field. It
was perhaps the most amazing moment of my
life — that and later hearing Pat Hughes
describe it as "beautifully sung by a lovely lady"
on WGN. that day proved to me, at 25,
that dreams can indeed come true.
   after all... that's what being a cubs fan
is all about, right?

            go cubs!   Jacky Dustin

Jacky, lead singer of The August
and two-time National Anthem performer
(Sept. 10, '07 and April 2, '08)

WE ARE CUBS FANS

WE ARE CUBS FANS

The year was 1984, the pavement was hot and the tickets being sold at Clark & Addison were scarce.

Positioned atop the most colorful circus I had ever seen, my dad told me to stick two hopeful fingers in the air.

"Like this," he said. I was five years old and sitting on his shoulders. I had never been to a Cubs game before.

We got into the game that day and more than 20 years later I will quit my job, move back to Chicago and plan to attend an entire season's worth of Cubs games the exact same way. Minus sitting on dad's shoulders, of course.

In 2006, my book "Wrigleyworld" came out and many people asked me where I got the idea. I always thought it was best to start at the beginning.

Kevin Kaduk

Go Cubs Go!

WRIGLEYWORLD
A Season in Baseball's Best Neighborhood
Kevin Kaduk

photo submitted by: Kevin Kaduk

WE ARE CUBS FANS

Celebrating a Cubs sweep on the porch of a building on Sheffield

WE ARE CUBS FANS

WHAT THE CUBS MEAN TO ME...

5/30/08

To be a Cubs fan is the most awesome thing there is. I cut myself & I bleed Cubby Blue, You should see it, it's amazing. I was born a Cubs fan & went to my 1st game when I was 3. A true Cubs fan knows there's Only One Chicago Team, and NEVER roots for anyone else, they would rather die. I recently had a decision to make, "My Senior Prom or The Cubs Game" guess what I picked?

Jamie
18
Des Plaines, IL

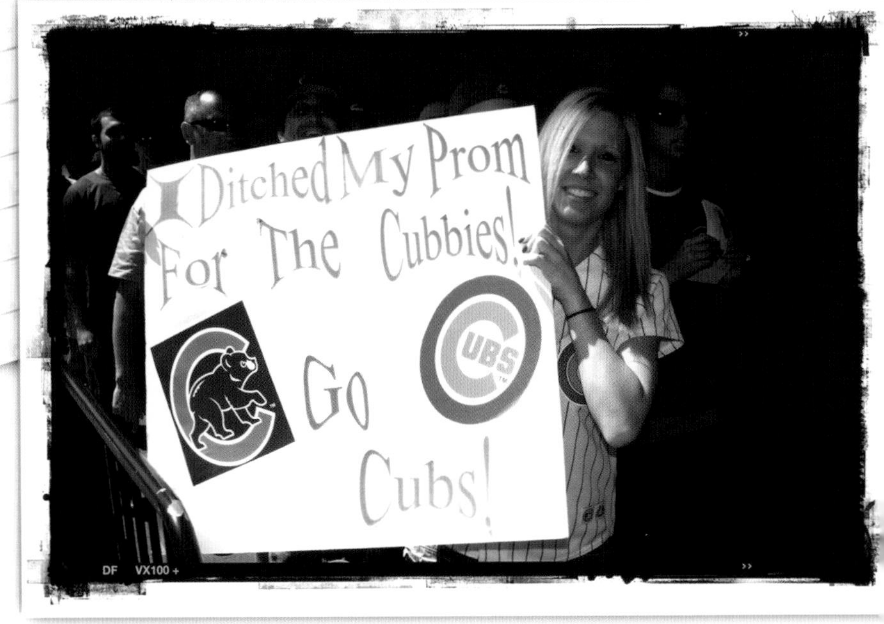

WE ARE CUBS FANS

WRIGLEY FIELD USED TO BE ONLY
A QUARTER FULL, THEREFORE THE SECURITY
GUARD WOULD MOVE MY FRIEND AND OUR MOMS
TO THE FIRST ROW BEHIND THE BULLPEN. AS
THE PLAYERS WARMED UP WE WOULD INTERACT WITH THEM, GET
AUTOGRAPHS, TAKE PHOTOS AND EVEN PLAY CATCH. ONE TIME DAVE KINGMAN
GAVE US MONEY TO BUY HIM SOME PEANUTS WHICH HE THEN GAVE BACK TO US.
WHILE SITTING SO CLOSE TO THE BULLPEN WE GOT TO KNOW BRUCE SUTTER AND HE
ATTENDED ONE OF MY LITTLE LEAGUE GAMES. THOSE MEMORIES ON THIS IMPRESSIONABLE
KID WILL KEEP ME A CUB FAN FOR LIFE.

BRYAN ANDERSON.

Lincoln Park Zoo

PO Box 14903
Cannon Drive at Fullerton Parkway
Chicago, Illinois 60614

Tel. 312-742-2000   Fax 312-742-2137

Bryan with Dave Kingman, 1978

WE ARE CUBS FANS

Bleeding Cubbie Blue in the Bleachers
Bottom row: Dave, Brian, Sue, Jeff Top row: Mark, Al, Phil

DF   VX100 +

WE ARE CUBS FANS

The Ultimate Cub Fan

My romance with the Cubs began in 1933 — I was three
I yelled at the top of my lungs "Weaver pitch strike 3"
Pat Flannagan was broadcasting — I've seen them all
Root, Hartnet, Cavaretta, Santo and Lee
Stan Hack was my idol, he played third base
His wonderful smile would light up my face
When I was nine I wished I were a boy
Then I could play for the Cubs — what a joy
The elusive World Series at Wrigley one day
Would cap off my dream of nearly a Century

Rosemary Libby

Ms Rosemary Libby

FAN SINCE 1933

WE ARE CUBS FANS

I ♥ THE CUBS
$ RON SANTO TOO!

WE ARE CUBS FANS

DF   VX100 +

WE ARE CUBS FANS

WHAT BEING A CUBS FAN MEANS TO ME

THE AWE OF SITTING IN THE BLEACHERS
AT WRIGLEY FIELD

KEEPING THE FAITH – EVEN WHEN ALL
HOPE SEEMS LOST

THE SPIRIT OF CUBS FANS ... EVERYWHERE

AND A COLD BUD LIGHT

Joe Scherder

DF   VX100 +

WE ARE CUBS FANS

DF   VX100 +

WE ARE CUBS FANS

" It's the fans that need spring training. You gotta get 'em interested.
Wake 'em up and let 'em know that their season is coming,
the good times are gonna roll."
Harry Caray, Hall of Fame Broadcaster

HARRY CARAY'S TAVERN

I was privileged to be part of the Cubs organization because of my late husband Harry Caray, a much loved announcer for The team. Since Harry passed in 1998, I've been overwhelmed by the outpouring of affection I've received from his fans. Everywhere I go, people tell me how much they loved and miss Harry — often with tears in their eyes. The Cubs have also done so much to keep Harry's memory alive. I love their tradition of having celebrities sing "Take Me Out To The Ballgame" — recognizing that no one person will ever replace Harry's special style of singing. I was both honored and terrified when they asked me to be the first guest singer after his passing. I was Harry would have loved our new Tavern across the street from Wrigley Field. He loved hanging out with the fans, and there's no better place to do that than Harry Caray's Tavern across the street from Wrigley Field.

This year, I was honored to be named Treasurer of the West Side Rooters Social Club, the revival of the first official fan Club of the Cubs. With Ernie Banks as Chairman Grant DePorter as President and Ryne Sandberg as Secretary - it's sure to be a lot of fun for all the fans. Let's hope that 2008 proves to be a great year for our Team. OOF WAH! (Go Cubs!)

Dutchie Caray

3551 North Sheffield • Chicago, IL 60657 • T: 773.327.7800 • F: 773.327.7842 • harrycaraystavern.com

(L to R) Grant, President
Dutchie, Treasurer
Ernie, Chairman
of the West Side Rooters
www.westsiderooters.com

WEST SIDE ROOTERS SOCIAL CLUB
OOF WAH
FOUNDED 1908

WE ARE CUBS FANS

WE ARE CUBS FANS

WE ARE CUBS FANS

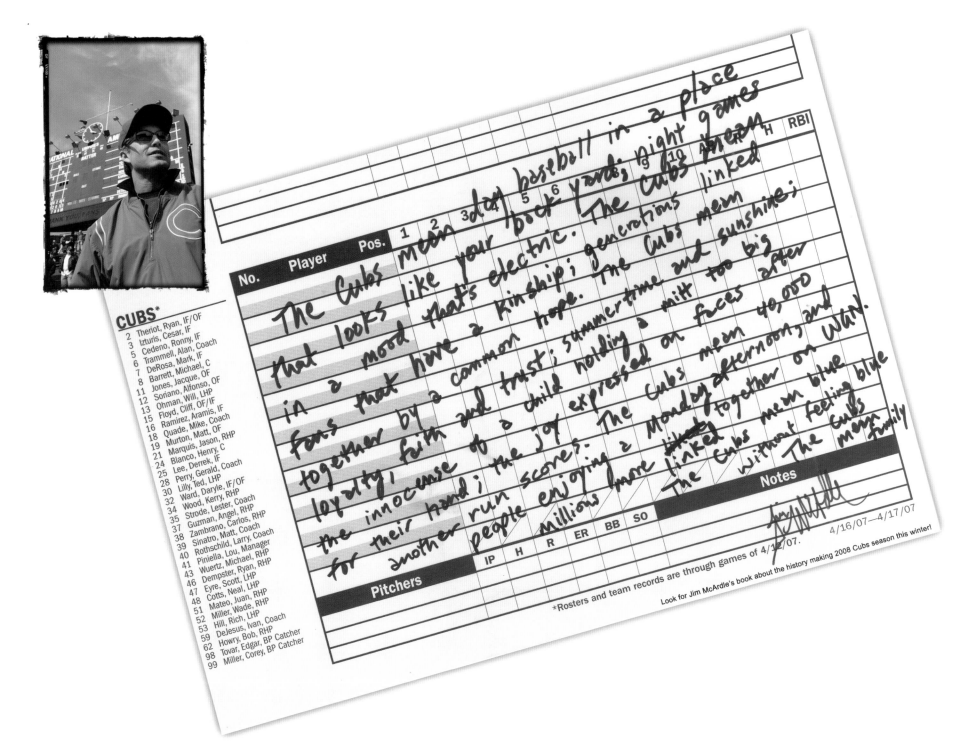

The Cubs mean 3 day baseball in a place that looks like your back yards; night games that's electric. The Cubs dream linked in a mood; generations. The Cubs mean fans that have a kinship; summertime and sunshine; together by a common hope. The Cubs mean loyalty, faith and trust; summertime and sunshine; the innocense of a child holding a mitt too big for their hand; the joy expressed on faces after another run scores. The Cubs mean 40,000 people enjoying a Monday afternoon, and linked together on WGN. The Cubs mean blue without feeling blue. The Cubs mean family

CUBS*

2 Theriot, Ryan, IF/OF
3 Izturis, Cesar, IF
5 Cedeno, Ronny, IF
6 Trammell, Alan, Coach
7 DeRosa, Mark, IF
8 Barrett, Michael, C
11 Jones, Jacque, OF
12 Soriano, Alfonso, OF
13 Ohman, Will, LHP
15 Floyd, Cliff, OF/IF
16 Ramirez, Aramis, IF
18 Quade, Mike, Coach
19 Murton, Matt, OF
21 Marquis, Jason, RHP
24 Blanco, Henry, C
25 Lee, Derrek, IF
28 Perry, Gerald, Coach
30 Lilly, Ted, LHP
32 Ward, Daryle, IF/OF
34 Wood, Kerry, RHP
35 Strode, Lester, Coach
37 Guzman, Angel, RHP
38 Zambrano, Carlos, RHP
39 Sinatro, Matt, Coach
40 Rothschild, Larry, Coach
41 Piniella, Lou, Manager
43 Wuertz, Michael, RHP
46 Dempster, Ryan, RHP
47 Eyre, Scott, LHP
48 Cotts, Neal, LHP
51 Mateo, Juan, RHP
52 Miller, Wade, RHP
53 Hill, Rich, LHP
59 DeJesus, Ivan, Coach
62 Howry, Bob, RHP
98 Tovar, Edgar, BP Catcher
99 Miller, Corey, BP Catcher

No.	Player	Pos.	1	2	3	4	5	6	7	8	9	10	AB	R	H	RBI

Pitchers	IP	H	R	ER	BB	SO	Notes

4/16/07—4/17/07

*Rosters and team records are through games of 4/12/07.

Look for Jim McArdle's book about the history making 2008 Cubs season this winter!

WE ARE CUBS FANS

WE ARE CUBS FANS

I have been a Cubs fan since meeting my husband, attending games & falling in love with Wrigley Field more than 14 years ago. Since then, my husband & I started a tradition of traveling to other ballparks to support the Cubs. We moved to Atlanta over 4 years ago & now, as the mother of 3 boys, I feel that it is my duty to continue the tradition & raise them to be loyal Cubs fans.

Chris McSherry

McSherry Family at Dolphins Stadium, 9/07

WE ARE CUBS FANS

WE ARE CUBS FANS

The Cubs have served as the backdrop of my life. Childhood memories are full of outings with my grandmother on "ladies day" or me and my dad holding our scorecards in one hand and wearing our mitts on the other. Lessons learned run the gamut from facing the flag during the national anthem to never putting ketchup on hotdogs!

I'm now passing these important lessons to my two daughters. They both have become fourth generation die-hards and always seem a little happier when the "W" flag is flying in front of our house.

David Selvy May

WE ARE CUBS FANS

Lt. Steve of the Chicago Fire Department Engine #78 on Waveland. Check out the tattoo!

WE ARE CUBS FANS

WE ARE CUBS FANS

WE ARE CUBS FANS

Yosh, Wrigley Field employee for 60+ years

WE ARE CUBS FANS

Despite the fact that Johnny and I were Sox fans and Mark, (we called him "Gus"), was a Cubs fan, we all got along real well. We met in grade school and have been friends ever since.

Recently, at the age of thirty-one, Gus lost a prolonged and courageous battle with cancer. His passing left a hole in many hearts — none bigger than those of his wife and two young boys.

As I think back about my buddy, there are three things I can state unequivocally about him: Gus loved his family, he loved his friends and he loved the Cubs.

Recognizing these things, I can smile now when I think about Gus. I take comfort knowing he's at peace, watching over the people he loved. And Cubs fans everywhere should also be comforted — because Heaven now has one more Angel singing, "Go Cubs Go! Go Cubs Go! Hey Chicago Whaddya Say?! The Cubs are gonna win today!"

Love you and miss you, Gus!

Mike

L-R: Mark (Gus), Johnny, Mike

WE ARE CUBS FANS

WE ARE CUBS FANS

WE ARE CUBS FANS

WHAT THE CUBS MEAN TO ME...

My dad and I have been coming to Cubs games for 53 years. The topic of conversation always includes The Cubbies whether we're here in Chicago or wherever I travels take us

We love our Cubbies

Please mail to:

Will B

3625

NAME: STEVE HEARN   FIRST CUBS GAME: 1955

DF VX100 +

WE ARE CUBS FANS

WE ARE CUBS FANS

WE ARE CUBS FANS

It's taking in 9 on a hot summer day in the bleachers, the hopes of every father who ever "took a catch" with his son, the little girl meticulously scribbling on her scorepad. It's the grin through tears of a man when the Cubs beat the Cardinals to clinch the pennant, the "W" flag flapping in the winds off Lake Michigan, the promise that maybe this year—hopefully this game—magic will happen & history will be made.

But mostly it's sharing a couple beers with my Dad, working our way through a bag of peanuts, talking about how the infield's looking.

We are Cubs fans.
—Niki Conrad

WE ARE CUBS FANS

Sitting with my family seven rows behind the bullpen in the summer of 1994. We walked up to the box office and bought the seats that morning. I was 13. My sister was 5. She jumps up and waved her little hand at my mom and I could do was stand there in awe. Luckly my dad had the camera in his hand and snapped this photo.

PS- I haven't lived at home with my parents for almost ten years now, but my mark grace poster is still on my bedroom door.

What the cubs mean to me... Great memories with my family!

- Amy Jo

photo submitted by: Amy Jo Chick

WE ARE CUBS FANS

WE ARE CUBS FANS

WE ARE CUBS FANS

WE ARE CUBS FANS

Ronnie, best known for his woo woo!

Cubito Ronnie   Love Every Body

Woo Life Happy   Cub Win

Love think good   Ronnie Woo

thought be nice   Woo

WE ARE CUBS FANS

FIRST CUBS GAME: April 5 1947

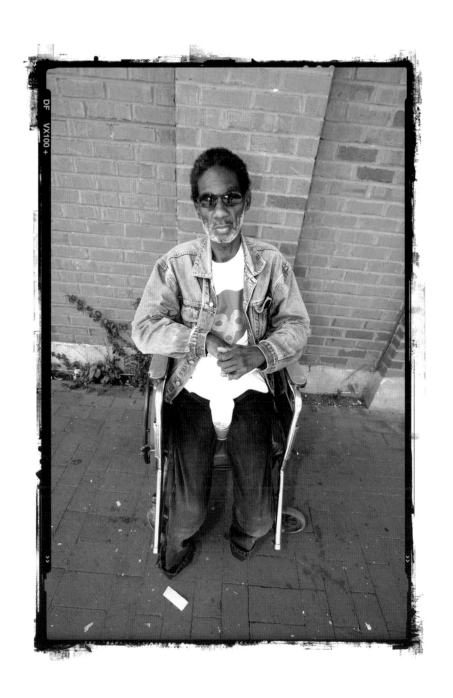

WE ARE CUBS FANS

WE ARE CUBS FANS

My name is Kate Keating. I am a nun and have been a Cub fan for almost 65 years. I knew I was a Cub fan before I knew I was Catholic! As a teacher for over 35 years, I always gave 2 extra points on students' work if they were Cub fans. I have attended many "at-home" playoff games. How? I take my lawn chair down to Addison and Sheffield and sit outside where I can see the scoreboard. I also have been to every championship celebration on Clark Street — no matter what time it started. I have suffered through '69, '84, '89, '98, '03 and '07. '84 and '03 were the toughest! My "wait until next year" and "in my lifetime" are running out. But I still live and die with the Cubs!

Kate Keating

WE ARE CUBS FANS

The Cubs, in many ways, present a snapshot of my life growing up in Lakeview!

• Ladies Day for 25¢.
• Waiting on Waveland Ave. for homerun balls — that's where the boys were!
• My brother-in-law sweeping the stands for free tickets.
• My dad teaching me to keep score the official way.
• My dad sitting in the bleachers for every home game after he retired — the only Cub fever kid in his south side neighborhood.
• Sharing Cub fever with my husband.
• Sharing Cub fever with a Cub jacket.
• Sharing Cub fever with our son and daughter.
• My hero — Ernie Banks!

Cindy Colaric

WE ARE CUBS FANS

WE ARE CUBS FANS

WE ARE CUBS FANS

There are only two reasons to get up before the sun rises:
1. boarding a plane headed for warmer weather
2. attending Opening Day at Wrigley Field

We got up that morning and made our way to Yakzies to join Lin Brehmer and the rest of WXRT to bring in Opening Day 2007. Over $5 Miller cans, we drank our breakfast while Robert Randolph serenaded us. We grabbed some Baccis before making our way down the street to HB where we cheered to steins with our German friends. We drank full grown men under the table before noon. Shortly thereafter we were in our favorite park, cheering our hearts out for our favorite team, the Cubs. I lost my voice and the Cubs lost the game that day, but Wrigleyville was alive and well as Cubs fans ventured back into the streets for continued shenanigans. This is where it starts to get a little blurry. Celia left with circa 12 beers in her to take a final that night, and we all made it home after another glorious opening day

"I Can Drink You Under the Table"
Celia and Meg

WE ARE CUBS FANS

DF   VX100 +

WE ARE CUBS FANS

WE ARE CUBS FANS

WE ARE CUBS FANS

photo submitted by: Joe Mantegna

Joe Mantegna

Being a Cubs fan falls into the category of character building. Here for the best and expect the worst. Are fine words to live by, and the Cubs are expect in grooming their fans to like a lifetime propelled by that phrase. Life is easy, comedy is hard ... and being a Cubs fan.

Joe Mantegna
Toluca Lake, CA.
6/4/08

WE ARE CUBS FANS

WE ARE CUBS FANS

The Cubs mean to me, waking up at 9:15am to move my car from Sheffield. Just to avoid the 4 hour before game time tow. They also mean Hebrew Nationals — mustard, grilled onions, kraut, where you wake up the next day with yellow mustard stains on your fingers and have no recollection of eating a hotdog. They also mean times like this — people lining up for tickets FOUR HOURS BEFORE GAMETIME. But hands down, my favorite Cubs experience is waking up the day after you go to a game and paying 50 cents for a Sun Times....JUST TO SEE WHO WON!

NAME: Bob Geniusz   FIRST CUBS GAME: APRIL 1988 vs. PIRATES

WE ARE CUBS FANS

What the Cubs mean to me can be summed up in two words, LASTING MEMORIES.

I remember my grandpa taking me to my first Cubs game and watching players like Ryne Sandberg, Andre Dawson, and Rick Sutcliffe.

I remember celebrating in the middle of the street with thousands of other fans when the Cubs won the NLC Division title in 2003.

I remember my husband, getting down on one knee and proposing to me under the famous Wrigley sign in 2004.
Lasting Memories...
The Cubs are in my blood!

Cub Fan For Life,

Katie Sherman

WE ARE CUBS FANS

WE ARE CUBS FANS

WE ARE CUBS FANS

I grew up in Joliet, 45 minutes from Chicago. I cried in October of 1984. I was 9. My dad, who'd just witnessed the Cubs first playoff appearance of his lifetime, probably told me to get used to it. He was only 32.

Now I'm 33, older than my dad was. I've seen the Cubs in the playoffs five times. In 2003 and 2007, I saw every Cubs playoff game, live at Wrigley Field. For free.

But how? Why? That's where I work. I get paid to be at Wrigley Field. To watch my beloved, tear-jerking Cubs. I hear the fans' unified roars and collective sighs. After each win, I join in, slap high-fives, and sing "Go Cubs Go."

My dreams as a kid were to patrol centerfield like Bob Dernier, diving on the green grass or into the even greener ivy. Now, as a grown man, I wear the same jersey and hat that Derrek Lee and Kerry Wood wear. I just happen to also wear cargo shorts, a three-pocketed apron, and blinding-white non-slip shoes. Lee and Wood play baseball on the field; I serve carrot cake and ice cream in the mezzanine suites.

But still, I work at Wrigley Field. Dreams can come true.

Go Cubs Go!

SCOTT DERENGER
SHAVEYOURHEAD.COM

WRIGLEY FIELD
HOME OF
CHICAGO CUBS
WELCOME TO
OPENING DAY 2008

WE ARE CUBS FANS

WE ARE CUBS FANS

I was born in 1946 and initially raised around Belmont and Damen avenues, a short stroll to Riverview and of course Wrigley Field. My Mother would always take us to Riverview on two cent Tuesdays and Wrigley Field for a Cubs game every Thursday for Ladies Day.

My brother and I grew up Cub fans and spent a lot of time at Wrigley Field. On our free days, we became part of the cup brigade. Here was the deal. At the end of the game, we ran around the stands and picked up all of the empty cups. Upon turning them in to a designated area, we were rewarded with a ticket for the next game. Then we would run to the players parking lot and gather in autographs. Every year we would get every player on the team. We had no interest in the visitors' autographs. Of course, as with baseball cards, the autograph books are long gone but the memories still exist.

I had the opportunity to play golf with Ernie Banks at the Hall of Fame Induction Ceremonies in Cooperstown. In fact, I rode, or should I say partially rode, in the cart with Ernie. Ernie played golf with the same enthusiasm as he played baseball.

On the first tee, he led the calisthenics before we teed off. Next, he informed me I would need to jog next to the golf cart every other hole. He drove pedal to the metal so it was not an easy stroll. By the way, Ernie jogged on the "other" every other hole.

Of course, upon shaking my hand at the end of eighteen, Ernie said "Let's Play Two". I could not handle a second round as I was exhausted.

Bob Anderson

Bob Anderson

WE ARE CUBS FANS

母の日
おめでとう
Happy Mother's
Day
GO CUBS!   GO CUBS!

MOTHERS ♥ their CUBS

GO CUBS
FELIZ
DIA DE LAS
MADRES
HARLINGEN ** TEXAS

DF   VX100 +

WE ARE CUBS FANS

What the Cubs mean to me...

I've been a Cubs fan for as long as I can remember. But that can hardly compare to my Grandfather, a die-hard fan for the past six decades. Even though he resides in Kentucky, he has remained the only die-hard Cubs fan in St. Louis Cardinal territory. When the local cable doesn't broadcast the games in his hometown, his trusty transistor radio allows him to never miss any of the seasons. He's braved snow and freezing temperatures at the opener last year, and has never gone a season without traveling to Chicago to see a game at Wrigley. My grandfather exemplifies what a true, passionate Cubs fan is. His enthusiasm has influenced me to be a loyal fan, and that dedication is a symbol of what the Cubs mean to me.

Sally Mjoseth

Lauren, Sally & Ashley at Wrigley

photo submitted by: Sally Mjoseth

WE ARE CUBS FANS

WE ARE CUBS FANS

WE ARE CUBS FANS

April 13th, 1984: Opening Day. My first Cubs game. Even at the mere age of 8 months, I must have developed a bond with the Cubs. My mom would tell me that one of my first words was "Cubs." When they played on WGN, I would stand up and sing the National Anthem. Everytime I would see the logo, I would scream "CUBS!" At 25 years old, I still get that feeling to shouts "Cubs!" But instead, I just think to myself "I'm so lucky to be a Cubs Fan."

Colleen M.

WE ARE CUBS FANS

WE ARE CUBS FANS

WHAT THE CUBS MEAN TO ME...

FOX VALLEY IL 605

15 MAR 2009PM 3 T

I love going to cubs games with my family because there's so much action! By:Drew

I love goining to the cubies game! Once Derrick Lee hit the cotton candy guy! I Love the cotton candy!

Matthew

Photograph submitted by: Kyle Berry

NAME: _Matthew, Age 6, Drew, Age 8._ **FIRST CUBS GAME:** _2006_

WE ARE CUBS FANS

DF   VX100 +

WE ARE CUBS FANS

When I think of the Cubs I think of my dad and my wife. Weird combo, I know. My dad worked the early shift at United Airlines for nearly 40 years. This meant afternoons where he was home in time to view every day game. There were times I remember my mom saying to him "I thought you were going to mow the yard today?", only to be met with "Harry (Caray) told me not to until the game was over." So for years after that, instead of my mom asking my dad why something wasn't done she would jump straight to "I suppose you didn't mow/vacuum/cle because Harry told you to watch the game?!"

Did my dad's passion for the team carry over to me? Ask my wi as she's the one whose wedding dress soaked up dirt when we had pictures taken in the Cubs dugout and on-deck circle the day we exchanged "I-Do's." As for me getting out of mowing the lawn... maybe when the Cubs win the series.

Go Cubs!!

Jeff Kearney

WE ARE CUBS FANS

Pat, Life long Cubs fan and building owner of the Budweiser house on Waveland checks out the view!

WE ARE CUBS FANS

"Wrigley is like another home in the community—when you're in Wrigley Field, it's like you're visiting the family of all the people that live around there."

– Hall of Famer, Mr. Cub Ernie Banks

WHAT THE CUBS MEAN TO ME ...

Well, I live in So. California, I Love coming to Wrigley Field to watch games (the best place to see a game). I'm a die hard Cubs fan, I never miss a game on T.V. the best thing about the cubs are the Loyal fans, (Best in Baseball I'll tell ya!) How could anyone not be a cubs fan. I would like to also say, It's Gonna Happen Baby!!

Jerry Sgt.

NAME: Jerry Sargent Jr.   FIRST CUBS GAME: August 2000

BREAST CANCER
FUND THE FIGHT, FUND A CURE

SANTA CLARITA C.
PM

W
362
CH

WE ARE CUBS FANS

WE ARE CUBS FANS

Holding my grandfather's hand as we walk thru Gate D. The smell of the grass brushing against my nose. Giving my xtra to the old guy in standing room. Believing good Guys finish 1st!

MARC ALGHINI

WE ARE CUBS FANS

I love the Cubs. Being a Cubs fan is who I am. I've loved them since the first game my dad took me to as a child. Wrigley is home; I don't think I've ever loved a place more then I love the Friendly Confines, and I can't imagine calling it anything else, but Wrigley Field. It's something about going there, knowing my grandparents saw games there, my dad & his siblings grew up going there, and he took me there. Every time I'm away, an ivy covered brick wall makes me think of being there. My dream of living at Wrigley Field finally came true this year. I might not live inside the Field, but Clark and Waveland is pretty close.

Eamus Catuli!

Ashley & Grant

CUBS Fan Since 1984

Being a Cubs fan has never been easy but since I was old enough to understand, I'd ask my Dad "Why are we Cubs fans, we never win?". It's because it means more to be a Cubs fan. Following a team like the Cubs can be an adventure. I used to dream about living steps away from Wrigley. I remember my first Cubs game in 1994 and getting my first autograph from "RYNO". I remember 1998 with Sammy captivating us all with his home run hop and sprint to right field at the start of every home game. I remember watching the games on WGN in the afternoon in the summer. Of all I remember 2003 and how close we got and being a freshman in college in Chicago for the first time. All of these memories are what makes a Cubs fan special and now that I've completed my dream of living steps from Wrigley! I'm ready for dream #1, winning it all.

Ashley and TJ at their apartment across from Wrigley

WE ARE CUBS FANS

Dorothy, season ticket holder and 7th inning stretch regular

WE ARE CUBS FANS

Family. It all started when I heard the story of my grandfather once jumping onto the roof of the dugout and cursing out Cubs manager Leo Durocher for a questionable decision. Naturally, my dad passed down that craze to his kids by raising us as Jack Brickhouse and Lou Boudreau and taking us into Chicago on the South Shore every summer. Now when I enter Wrigley, I carry those fond memories and experiences of the Cubs and my family with me. To my beautiful daughters and patient wife - hopefully this helps explain why I feel the way I do about my Cubbies.

— Kevin Quinn

WE ARE CUBS FANS

WE ARE CUBS FANS

THE CHICAGO CUBS ARE NOT JUST
A BASEBALL TEAM. THE CHICAGO
CUBS ARE ME LEARNING HOW TO
KEEP SCORE AT A BALL GAME
WITH MY GRANDFATHER WHEN I WAS
YOUNG. THEY ARE THE THOUGHT THAT
NO MATTER HOW BAD IT GETS, THERE
WILL BE GOOD THINGS TO COME.
THEY ARE THE MEMORIES OF ME
AND MY FATHER, FRIENDS, AND
SOME DAY OF ME AND MY CHILDREN.
THEY ARE A BEAUTIFUL SUMMER DAY
AND THEY COME ALONG WITH OUR DAILY
LIVES. THE CHICAGO CUBS HAVE
ALWAYS BEEN THERE DURING SOME
OF THE GREATEST MEMORIES OF MY
LIFE, AND SOME OF THE WORST. THEY
ARE A BEST FRIEND BECAUSE YOU CAN
ALWAYS COUNT ON THEM TO BE
THERE FOR YOU.

TOM LISACK

WE ARE CUBS FANS

MY 1st CUBS GAME!

5.10.08

WE ARE CUBS FANS

Vince, Hollywood Actor and Chicago native

WE ARE CUBS FANS

WHAT THE CUBS MEAN TO ME...

It was a Sunday night in August, the fourth of four with those Cardinals, when sheer chance landed us on a Sheffield rooftop at twilight. The city sprawled at our feet as dying light and purpling prairie converged. Wrigley sparkled below, jewel-like - in a tight, tense game not decided until the ninth when Albert Pujols stranded the go-ahead runs. Down on the stoop, still jazzed, we gushed baseball into the night: me, my friends, and my two sons. Then Wild Bill, too (!), finally finished his long walk.

Even now the memory of that night fills my heart and jumps my throat.

Rich Megraw

Megraw Boys on a Sheffield Rooftop

WE ARE CUBS FANS

What the Cubs Mean to Me

Central Division
Losing with precision
For 100 years
'Bleacher Bums' with beers
The 'North Siders'
Smile Providers
Wrigley Field since 1916
Starring Harry Caray and ivy so green
First night game in '88
WGN, Maddux, a fan base so great
Cubby Blue
Ronnie Woo Woo
"W" flag soaring
'Friendly Confines' roaring
Santo, Sandberg, Williams and Banks
Sosa and Fukudome (to whom we give thanks)
Lee Elia, Lou Pinella
Kerry Wood...just stay healthy fella
Billy Goat Curse and "The Bartman Play"
Hey Hey... the Cubs are gonna win today

David E. Feld

WE ARE CUBS FANS

WE ARE CUBS FANS

"People ask me what I do in the winter when there's no baseball?
I'll tell you what I do, I stare out the window and wait for spring!"

Rogers Hornsby, Chicago Cubs 1929-1932

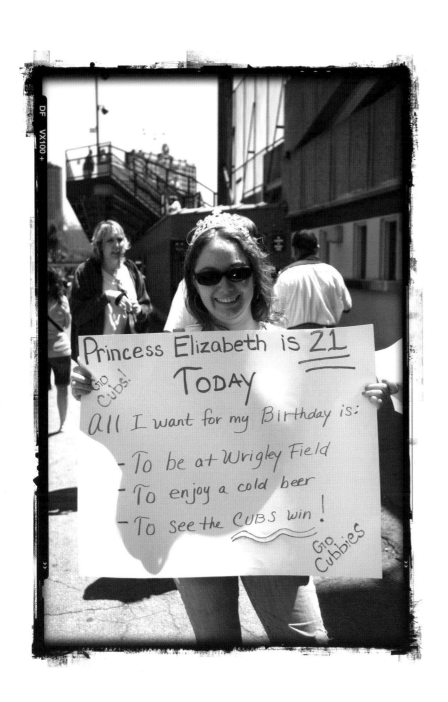

Princess Elizabeth is 21
TODAY
All I want for my Birthday is:
- To be at Wrigley Field
- To enjoy a cold beer
- To see the CUBS win!

Go
Cubs!

Go
Cubbies

Smack that ball hard
Cubs
go cubs go

WE ARE CUBS FANS

THERE ARE "86" MORE DAYS 'TIL NEXT YEAR!
The Bleacher Preacher
OCTOBER 6,2007

BLEACHER PREACHER

Jerry, The Bleacher Preacher

I always equated my youth, with Cubs Tea from the mid-1940's and 50's! In 1945, I was 8 years old. My Dad gave me a crash cours in Baseball 101, Cubs History, Baseball Traditions and Keeping a scorecard. Then I went to my 1ST Cubs game at Beautifu Wrigley Field. IT was "MAJESTIC"!

Baseball was the Official Language at the Pritikin kitchen Table. Going to the Ballpark on the Big Red Street Cars... Getting Off at Clark & Addison. Andy Frai Ushers in their "crisp" Uniforms. The Friendl Voices of Pat Pieper & P-nut Vendor Gravi Gertie... the "W" at the end of the game and Always The Hope

This is THE YEAR!

Jerry Pritikin
AKA The Bleacher Preacher

WE ARE CUBS FANS

WE ARE CUBS FANS

To be a Cubs fan is the proudest of groups in which to belong… it is a special calling. One not for the faint of heart or the weak-willed. At the very essence is a spirit that thrives on hope…and dreams…and believing that the impossible is possible! To be at Wrigley Field is to breathe in the flavor of an historic place… it is a heady combination of determination, courage, victory and defeat all grilled together and served on a bun accompanied by a cold one.

The bats at Wrigley swing to a pulse that is Chicago…balls catapulted past the 400 sign in center field caressed and lifted by the gentle breeze (or occasional gale) that blows off Lake Michigan . The synergy of the Cubs players and the cheering fans builds a positive energy, deafening at times, that resonates throughout the ballpark and overflows into the streets of Clark, Sheffield, Waveland, and Addison…every Cubs fan buoyed by the experience…and never the same after having felt it. "Might be…could be…IT IS…OUR year!! Go CUBS GO!!"
- Georgia Hammerli (via e-mail)

Being a Cubs fan means being the envy of the entire league. Cubs means the friendly confines at Wrigley Field, Sold out Tuesday day games, and gas bump inducing passion. It means nine different kind of hotdog, peanuts, their salty shells, and the beloved Beer Man. A Cubs game means my girlfriend in her child's size large DeRosa Jersey; hoarse from laughing and screaming at the opposing teams left fielder.

With my Cardinals fan Grandfather, who never lets us miss a series, my midweek/day game loving father, and my rabid Cub fan Girlfriend, we say: "Cubs are gonna win today!"
—Steven Peterson

CUBDOM Inbox | X

Dick Schroeder to me   show details May 27   ↰ Reply | ▼

In February my high school buddies gave me a new Cubs jersey with SCHROEDER and 80 on the back (for my age).The reason: We all graduated from Lake View H.S. and are still dedicated to OUR CUBS.
I attended the 1935 and 1938 world series with my father, and the 1945 with my school buddies. My favorite all-time Cub was Billy Herman, followed closely by Ernie Banks. Highlites for me was attending three NO-Hitters (the best one when Sam Jones walked the first three hitters in the ninth, and then struck out the next three on nine pitches).
No matter what happens…It's GREAT to be a CUB FAN!
Ghetto Dick

↰ Reply ↰ Reply to all → Forward

WE ARE CUBS FANS

I have yet to find a prouder group of people than Chicagoans of their Cubs, and I feel honored to be a part of that. It has, and always will be, in my blood. I AM A CHICAGO CUBS GIRL!

Jenny Schmitt

Memories That Last Forever - Holding my Dad's ticket and scorecard from the Cubs/Yankees world series game when the Babe "called the called shot". Sitting in the bleachers with family and friends during snow, wind, rain, cold, and heat all the while hoping the Cubs would win, enduring the failures of so many players we thought were going to get us to the promised land, watching the final "complete" night game with a longtime friend. The atmosphere was something I will always cherish. Harry the fortune to watch so many Cubs legends - Santo, Banks, Sandberg, Williams, Jenkins, Sandberg.

NAME: **CHUCK GATZ** FIRST CUBS GAME: EARLY '50's

It turns out the Cubs are an addiction. Really. You don't realize it at first. You start going to five or six games then it's twenty, and then next thing you know you're making forty or fifty games each year and planning your life around their schedule.
But now that I've figured out the addiction angle
I'm going to get some help, get it under control, and cut back on the games.
Right after we win the Series….

Tom Evans (via e-mail)

I'm five years old, and it's Ernie Banks' last season. My dad takes me to Wrigley to see Mr. Cub play one last time. But Durocher has soured on Banks. My dad's nervous, real nervous, that Durocher will sit Banks. That nervousness. That anticipat. That hope. That rarified Wrigley Field air. That grin of my dad's when Ernie's name is announced. That shared affection for something, anything, that will last as long as we do.
Donald J Evans
May 7, 2008

One of my first childhood memories of my dad is his week routine of settling into his comfy recliner and turning the to the Cubs game. He always invited me hop into the recli and watch the game with him. Sometimes he nodded o for a few innings, but he always woke up in time to see the He was a man of few words; sharing his only quiet time wit was very special. I wanted to share that connection with my so as soon as they were toddlers we started bringing them to W We have great memories of being in the park, cheering on the watching home runs, eating hot dogs, foul balls never landing enough to catch, and bees attacking!

Today those toddlers are 20 and 23 and we still go to see the Cubs together as a family.

Wendy Hayum-Gross (via e-mail)

Angelo G.
Aspira

JOURNAL   5-23-08
                                6th

The cubs to me means more than just a regular team, it means of how the game is played and how much we love it. It's not only about winning, it's about playing fair and getting respect from other teams. Whenever I'm in any stadium, I see the fans cheering, meeting new friends, and having a great time. But when I'm at Wrigley Field, you feel something in you that is just like watching the firewor on the fourth of July and being with your family on New Years' Eve altogether.

favorite day of the year is pening Day. From that point on, I know I get to follow the Cubs for 162 thrilling games. The highs and lows of every Cubs season fuel me through the summer. My obsession has even taken me to the road: San Fran, LA, San Diego, Mesa, Houston, Pittsburgh, Milwaukee and Cincinnati - done. But nothing beats the Friendly Confines and the history that it holds. The ivy, the atmosphere, the CUBS! I will be a loyal fan forever.

NAME: Neal Glassett **FIRST CUBS GAME:** 1985 - age 7

---

steven weissmann to me   show details May 27   ↩ Reply | ▼

What the Cub's mean to me:

The Cub's for me, represent the promise of something special. I have always felt as though they are like the perfect girl in high school. She was the captain of the cheerleading squad, beautiful and sexy, yet virtue intact. She smiles at me (a winning season, with hope), flirts with me every once in a while (a playoff berth), always keeping my hopes alive. While I fantasize about the glory that I might find one day with her, I also know deep down that the fantasy, may well be greater than any reality that might be realized. How I do love the fantasy though.

Steven Weissmann

↩ Rep

The Cubs symbolize loyalty to me. A true fan is loyal to the end. It means walking around Wrigleyville "high fiving" everyone when they win and consoling everyone when they lose. At the end of the season, I have a feeling of loss because I won't see my Boys in Blue for awhile but I know they'll always be back. The Cubs are a part of my life and always will be.

Cheers to the Boys in Blue!

Cindy

NAME: Cindy McGuire **FIRST CUBS GAME:** July, 1988

, I'm a Cubs addict. For ty-three years. Wrigley's a magical are where dreams come true. At east for one afternoon. It's intimate, wonderfully old-fashioned. Like returning to another era when baseball was played on a verdant field, sun shining, green vines hugging the walls.

What an electric feeling saluting the flag within a large community. Everyone here for a common goal, a victory. No one cares about race, religion or age.

CUBS WIN!!! The whole world — for just one minute - is perfect. Nothing exists except happiness that is shared by forty thousand people.

The Cubs mean hope to me.

Patt Rutter

What it means to be a Cubs fan: the only people in the entire world I have loved more than my parents are the Chicago Cubs. It's a family. You stand on your feet in April or September, cheer as loud as you can, and wear that Cubs "C" with pride. You argue with grown adults (if you can call Sox & Cardinals fans adults) about a baseball team... your baseball team. Your able to be apart of something that no matter what age, race, or religion you are everyone comes together for one common thing: to see the Cubs win. You can't pick your family & sometimes not even your friends, but you can PICK who you cheer for & I pick the Chicago Cubs!

NAME: Megan Stevens **FIRST CUBS GAME:** June 1998

HOPE: That is what the Cubs mean to me. In a WORLD FULL OF DISEASE AND WAR, the Cubs give me hope. You may wonder how a team that hasn't won a WORLD SERIES In 100 years CAN give someone hope, to understand this it helps to look at what hope is. HOPE implies a certain amount of despair, WANTING, WISHING, SUFFERING or PERSEVERANCE, IT IS BELIEVING that a BETTER or POSITIVE OUTCOME IS POSSIBLE EVEN when there is SOME EVIDENCE TO THE CONTRARY. To Me - that is what being a CUBS FAN is.

YEAR IN, YEAR OUT....

HOPE

— Matthew Campobasio
MAY 26, 2008

"Hey, I have an extra ticket to the Cubs game. It's yours if you want it." Oh, how I love to hear that phrase! Whatever my responsibilities are that day, whatever work is piled up, whatever errands must be run, however angry my girlfriend will be to hear about me attending another game, the blissful experience of Wrigley Field takes first priority. Every Cubs game is a vacation, and Wrigley Field is the best resort money can buy (if only it were all-inclusive!). You can keep your Hawaiian Islands and Caribbean cruises, Clark and Addison is my preferred destination."

Dan Zarlenga (via e-mail)

WE ARE CUBS FANS

WHAT THE CUBS MEAN TO ME...

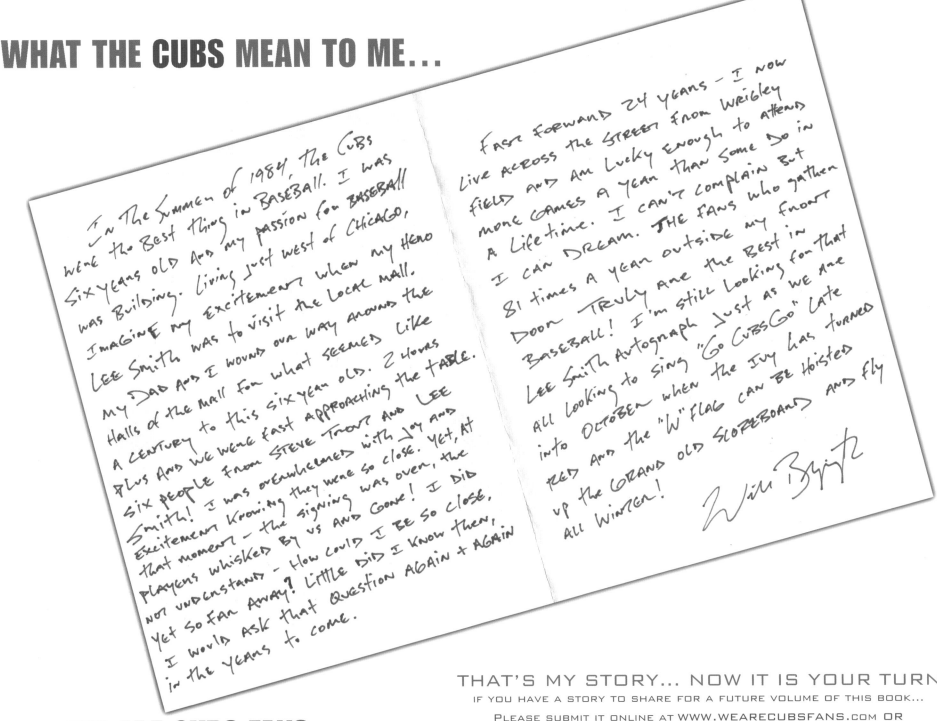

In The Summer of 1984, The Cubs were the Best thing in BASEBALL. I was Six years old And my passion for BASEBALL was Building. Living Just west of CHICAGO, Imagine my excitement when my Hero Lee Smith was to visit the local mall. My Dad and I wound our way around the Halls of the mall for what seemed Like A Century to this six year old. 2 Hours Plus and we were fast approaching the table. Six people from Steve Trout and Lee Smith! I was overwhelmed with Joy and excitement knowing they were so close. Yet, At that moment — the signing was over, the players whisked By us and Gone! I did not understand — How could I Be so close, yet so far Away? Little did I know then, I would Ask that Question AGAIN + AGAIN in the years to come.

Fast forward 24 years — I now live across the street from wrigley field And Am lucky enough to attend more games a year than some Do in A lifetime. I can't complain But I can Dream. The fans who gather 81 times a year outside my front Door Truly Are the Best in Baseball! I'm still looking for that Lee Smith Autograph Just as we Are All looking to sing "Go Cubs Go" Late into October when the ivy has turned Red And the "W" flag can Be Hoisted up the GRAND OLD scoreboard and fly all winter!

Will Bryant

WE ARE CUBS FANS

For me, the Cubs mean road trips
spent with my whole family listening
to static on the radio. All for the
small chance that we might be
able to pick up the Cubs' game on
the WGN-AM station....from Florida.

Kelly Coyle
Age 29

LIKE WHAT YOU SEE?

HAVE A STORY TO SHARE?

SUBMIT IT NOW FOR

VOLUME #2 OF

WE ARE CUBS FANS

PLEASE HANDWRITE YOUR STORY IN UNDER 200 WORDS ANSWERING THE QUESTION:

WHAT THE CUBS MEAN TO ME

SUBMIT ONLINE AT WEARECUBSFANS.COM OR BY THE US POSTAL SERVICE

* INCLUSION OF PHOTOS OR LETTERS IS AT THE SOLE DISCRETION OF WILL BYINGTON AND IS FINAL. SUBMISSION OF LETTERS AND ORIGINAL PHOTOS WILL NOT BE RETURNED AND PERMISSION IS GRANTED BY ALL PARTIES CAPTURED WITHIN PICTURES OR LETTERS FOR POSSIBLE USE IN ANY FUTURE VOLUME OF THE WE ARE CUBS FANS SERIES.

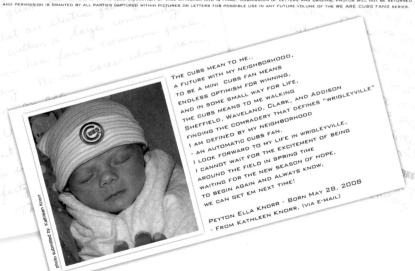

THE CUBS MEAN TO ME..
A FUTURE WITH MY NEIGHBORHOOD,
TO BE A MINI CUBS FAN MEANS
ENDLESS OPTIMISM FOR WINNING,
AND IN SOME SMALL WAY FOR LIFE,
THE CUBS MEANS TO ME WALKING
SHEFFIELD, WAVELAND, CLARK, AND ADDISON
FINDING THE COMRADRY THAT DEFINES "WRIGLEYVILLE"
I AM DEFINED BY MY NEIGHBORHOOD
- AN AUTOMATIC CUBS FAN.
I LOOK FORWARD TO MY LIFE IN WRIGLEYVILLE,
I CANNOT WAIT FOR THE EXCITEMENT OF BEING
AROUND THE FIELD IN SPRING TIME
WAITING FOR THE NEW SEASON OF HOPE,
TO BEGIN AGAIN AND ALWAYS KNOW,
WE CAN GET EM NEXT TIME!

PEYTON ELLA KNORR - BORN MAY 28, 2008
- FROM KATHLEEN KNORR, (VIA E-MAIL)

photo submitted by Kathleen Knorr

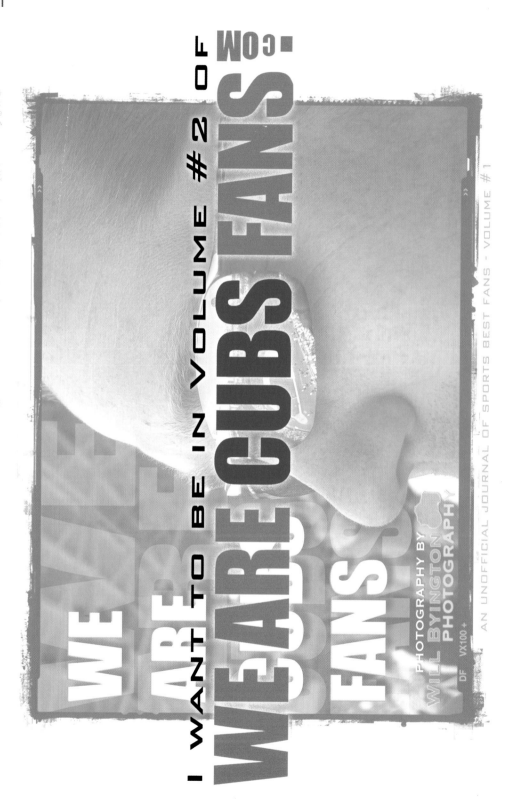

PLEASE HANDWRITE YOUR STORY IN UNDER 200 WORDS ANSWERING THE QUESTION:

WHAT THE CUBS MEAN TO ME...

SUBMIT ONLINE AT WEARECUBSFANS.COM OR BY THE US POSTAL SERVICE

* INCLUSION OF PHOTOS OR LETTERS IS AT THE SOLE DISCRETION OF WILL BYINGTON AND IS FINAL. SUBMISSION OF LETTERS AND ORIGINAL PHOTOS WILL NOT BE RETURNED AND PERMISSION IS GRANTED BY ALL PARTIES CAPTURED WITHIN PICTURES OR LETTERS FOR POSSIBLE USE IN ANY FUTURE VOLUME OF THE WE ARE CUBS FANS SERIES

Please mail to:

Will Byington
c/o We Are Cubs Fans
P.O. Box 5397
Naperville, IL
60567-5397

WE ARE CUBS FANS .COM
WWW.WEARECUBSFANS.COM

My eternal optimism is owed to the Cubs (and my optimistic mother). You learn quickly as a life-long Cub fan to always look to the brighter side of life because we were forced to. (I feel for my father's 60 years of optimism.) My dad always coached little league when we were kids, and we always won. In some bizarre way the Cubs kept us all grounded because no matter how well we played on the field, we still lost because the Cubs did.

You learn confidence without cockiness. We knew that even though the Cubs may start off the season playing well that we couldn't get cocky because we knew our history. We in return learned how to make the best of being the underdogs by embracing the culture involved in being Cub fans. Cub fans love each other because we have all experienced the same heartbreaks and hangovers.

When I started liking boys in Jr. High being a Cubs fan was a prerequisite and my first celebrity crush was Mark Grace.

It's those moments now when we are scattered across the country and the Cubs bring us back together to scream and yell because no one else really understands why you're so excited. (Or frustrated when we're losing.)

It's a culture that can't be known unless you've lived it. The Cubs are much more than a baseball team they are a part of our families and our upbringing.

But this our time to be winners and our time to feel some glory...GO CUBS!!!

Jessica Bertulis (via e-mail)

photo submitted by Jessica Bertulis

FIRST CUBS GAME:

Angelo G.
Aspira

Alert   3:16am

New Text Message
From: MegsKeenan

good times + bad beer
with friends = chicago
cubs games. lol.
go cubs go.

<3 meg